W0013561

ELEVEN CHORALE PRELUDES

opus 122

Brahms

Order No: NOV 590116

NOVELLO PUBLISHING LIMITED
8/9 Frith Street, London W1V 5TZ

EDITORIAL NOTE

THESE Eleven Chorale Preludes were composed by Brahms at Ischl, Upper Austria, in May and June, 1896, during the last year of his life, and were issued posthumously.

In the present edition the notes for right and left hands have been clearly differentiated, either by re-staving where convenient, or by the indications *R.H.* and *L.H.*, and Brahms's use of the alto clef in certain passages has been discarded.

The time indications, dynamic marks, etc., given in the original edition have been retained, but all suggested modifications of these, or additions to them, will be found enclosed in brackets. In the more expressive passages a number of Swell pedal crescendos and diminuendos will suggest themselves to experienced players. It has been considered inadvisable, however, to add these and other details which are best left to the discretion of the performer.

Changes of manual formerly indicated as *Man. I.*, *Man. II.*, etc., have here been translated into suggested terms of *Gt.*, *Ch.*, *Sw.*, etc., but the choice of stops is left to the player, except in a few specific cases. One or two slight alterations have been made in the position of a manual change, for the sake of a better effect. These occur in No. VII, *O Gott, du frommer Gott*, page 21, bar 5; page 22, bar 17; and page 23, bar 12. Further suggestions have been made incidentally by means of foot notes.

The somewhat intermittent use of phrasing slurs has been left almost entirely as given in the original. A few of them have been slightly modified in length and others have been added here and there in order to be consistent. It must be assumed, however, that the discontinuance of slurs by no means indicates that the music ceases to be legato.

An English translation of the German text of the chorales has been provided.

October 1928

JOHN E. WEST

CONTENTS

		PAGE
I	MEIN JESU, DER DU MICH ('My Jesus calls to me')	1
II	HERZLIEBSTER JESU ('O Blessed Jesu')	8
III	O WELT, ICH MUSS DICH LASSEN ('O world, I now must leave thee')	10
IV	HERZLICH THUT MICH ERFREUEN ('My faithful heart rejoices')	13
V	SCHMÜCKE DICH, O LIEBE SEELE ('Deck thyself, my soul')	16
VI	O WIE SELIG SEID IHR DOCH, IHR FROMMEN ('Blessed are ye faithful souls')	18
VII	O GOTT, DU FROMMER GOTT ('O God, Thou faithful God')	20
VIII	ES IST EIN' ROS' ENTSPRUNGEN ('Behold, a rose is blooming')	24
IX	HERZLICH THUT MICH VERLANGEN ('My heart is filled with longing') First Setting	26
X	HERZLICH THUT MICH VERLANGEN ('My heart is filled with longing') Second Setting	28
XI	O WELT, ICH MUSS DICH LASSEN ('O world, I now must leave thee')	32

I

MEIN JESU, DER DU MICH

My Jesus calls to me

Johannes Brahms, Op. 122, Book 1

[Con moto moderato]
MANUAL
(m)f ma dolce
Gt. (Sw. coupled)
L. H.
PEDAL

My
Mein
f 16 & 8 ft. (Gt. & Sw. coupled)

Je - - - sus
Je - - - su,
calls
der
to
du
me,
mich
L.H.
(cresc.)
(più f)
Holds
zum

out
Lust - - Spiel
e - - - ter - - - - nal
e - - . - wig - -
bliss.
- lich.
p Sw.
(G! to Ped. in)
L.H.
He
dir
mp

deigns
hast
to
er
choose
wäh
me.
let,
P Ch.(Sw. coupled)
Ch.
(cresc. poco a poco)
Hear,
Sieh'
mp (Ch. to Ped.)

Lord,
wie
Thy
dein
ser - - vant
Ei - - gen - -
meek
- thum
(m)f Gt
(L.H.)
R.H.
Sings
des
f (Gt to Ped.)

loud the Bride - - groom's
gro - - ssen Bräut' - - gams

praise,
Ruhm

f (add)

In
so

(increase gradually)
Thee re - - - - joi - - - - - - -
gern er - - - - zäh - - - - - - -

(rit. poco a poco al fine)
(ff)
- ces. [Trs. M. D. Calvocoressi]
- let.

II

HERZLIEBSTER JESU

O Blessed Jesu

O bless - ed Je - su, how hast
Herz - lieb - ster Je - su, was hast
Adagio
MANUAL
PEDAL
f Gt
f 16 & 8 ft. (Gt & Sw. coupled)

Thou of - fend - ed, That
du ver - bro - chen, dass

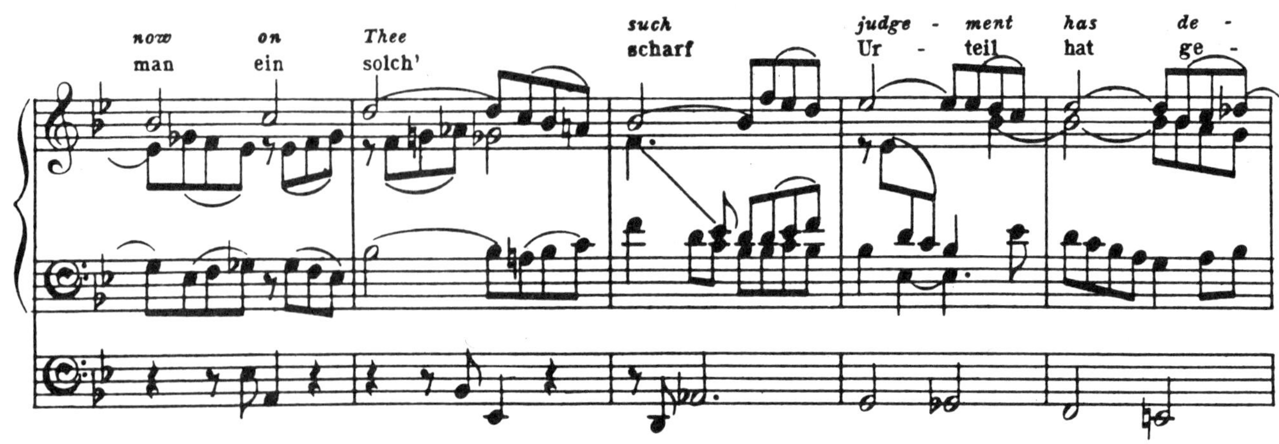
now on Thee such judge - ment has de -
man ein solch' scharf Ur - teil hat ge -

-scend - - ed? Of what mis - deed
- spro - - chen? Was ist die Schuld?
Sw.
Sw.
p
p
(Gt to Ped. in)
hast Thou to make con - fes - - - -
in was für Mis - se - tha - - - -
cresc.
p
-sion? Of what trans - gres - - - -
- ten bist du ge - - ra - - - -
Gt
Gt
f
f
(Gt to Ped.)
- sion? [Trs. Dr J. Troutbeck]
- then?
R.H.
(rit.)

III

O WELT, ICH MUSS DICH LASSEN

O world, I now must leave thee

[Larghetto con moto]
O
O
world,
Welt,
I
ich
MANUAL
Gt (mf) ma dolce
PEDAL
(m)f 16 & 8 ft (Gt coupled)
now
muss
must
dich
leave
las -
thee,
- sen,
And
ich
go
fahr
my lone
da - hin
- ly
mein
jour
Stra
- ney
- ssen

To my e - ter - nal
ins ew'- ge Va - ter -

R.H.

home. I faith - - - ful -
-land. Mein Geist will

-ly and hum - bly Com -
ich auf - ge - ben, da -

-mit my soul and bo - dy
-zu mein Leib und Le - ben

(m)*f* (Sw.)

(Gt to Ped in.
Sw. coupled)

un - to the Lord's
be - fehl'n in Got -

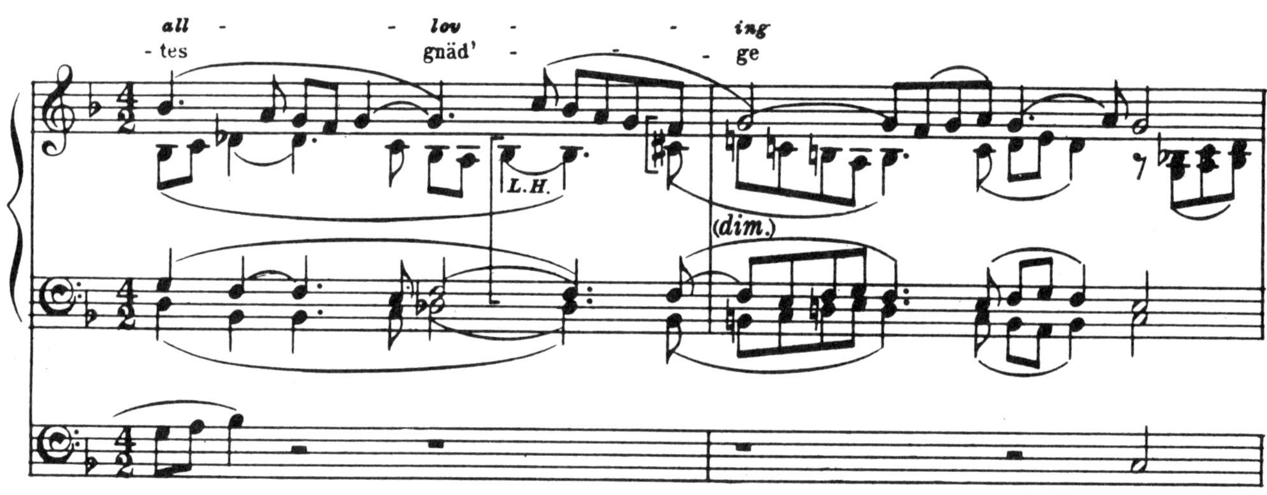
all - lov - ing
- tes gnäd' - - ge
L.H.
(dim.)

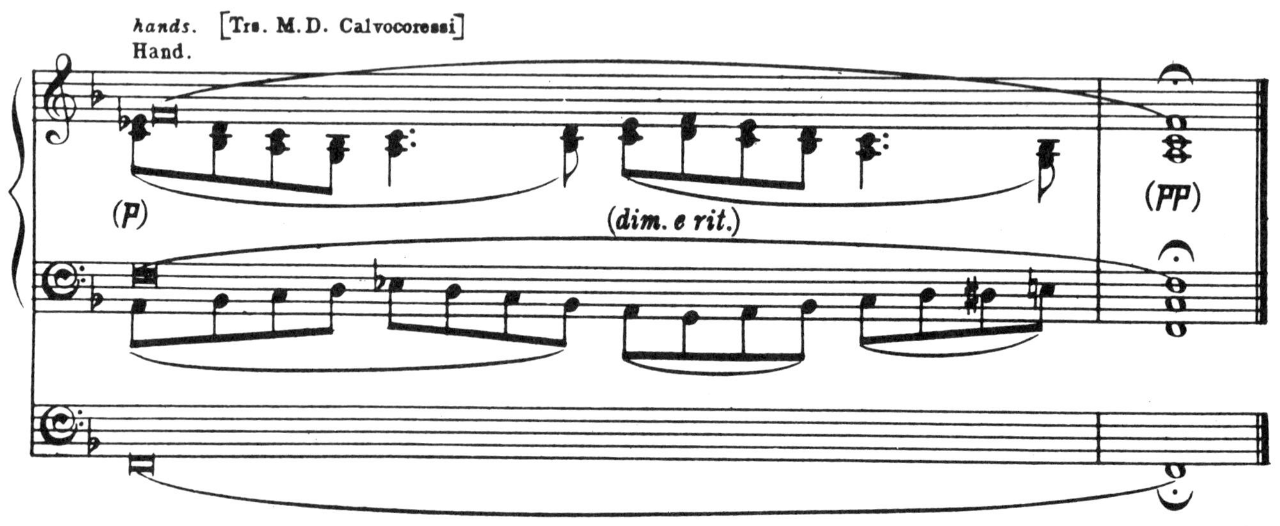
hands. [Trs. M.D. Calvocoressi]
Hand.
(P)
(dim. e rit.)
(PP)

IV

HERZLICH THUT MICH ERFREUEN

My faithful heart rejoices

[Allegro moderato]
Sw.
mf dolce
Sw.
MANUAL
PEDAL

My faith - ful heart re -
Herz - lich thut mich er -
f Gt
f 16 & 8 ft (Gt coupled)

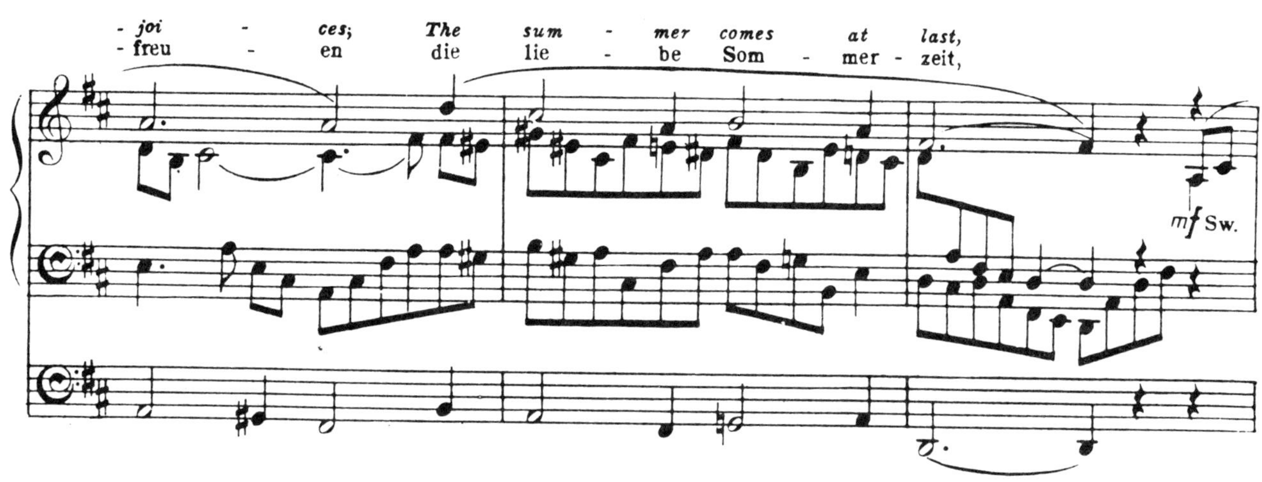
- joi - ces; The sum - mer comes at last,
- freu - en die lie - be Som - mer - zeit,
mf Sw.

When God, all things re - viv - ing, Shall
wann Gott wird schön ver - neu - en al -
f Gt
f
bring E - ter - ni - ty.
- les zur E - wig - keit,
p Ch. (or Sw.)
The
Den
f Gt
f

Heav'n and Earth in splen - dour Will He a - fresh cre -
Him - mel und die Er - den wird Gott neu schaf - fen
-ate,
gar,
Sw.
p
Ch.(or Sw.)
And all of us, His
all Cre - a - tur soll
f Gt
f
crea - tures, Shall pure and flaw - less be.
wer - den ganz herr - lich, hübsch und klar.
[Trs. M.D. Calvocoressi]
(rit.)

V

SCHMÜCKE DICH, O LIEBE SEELE

Deck thyself, my soul

Johannes Brahms, Op. 122, Book 2
[Andante moderato]
Deck thy - self, my soul, with glad - ness,
Schmü-cke dich, o lie - be See - le,
MANUAL
Ch(or Gt)
p dolce (c legato)
Leave the gloom - y haunts of sad - -
lass die dunk - le Sün - den - höh - -
- ness, Come in - to the day - light's
- le, komm ans hel - le Licht ge -
splen - - - dour, There with joy thy
- gan - - - gen, fan - ge herr - lich
prais - es rend er Un - to
an zu pran - gen! Denn der

Him Whose grace un - bound - - ed
Herr voll Heil und Gna - - den

Hath this wond rous ban - quet found -
will dich jetzt zu Ga - ste la -

-ed, High o'er all the heavn's He
den; der den Him - mel kann ver -

reign - - eth, Yet to dwell with
-wal - - ten, will jetzt Her - berg

thee He deign - - eth. [Trs. Catherine Winkworth]
in dir hal - - ten.

(*rit.*)

VI

O WIE SELIG SEID IHR DOCH, IHR FROMMEN

Blessed are ye faithful souls

Johannes Brahms Op.122, Book 2

Molto moderato
Bless - - - ed
O wie
are ye, faith - - ful
se - lig seid ihr
MANUAL
Gt (mp) dolce (e legato)

souls de - - part - - - ed;
doch, ihr From - - - men,

Death a - - - - wak - - ened you to
die ihr durch den Tod zu
R.H.

life im - mor - - tal.
Gott ge - - kom - - - men,
You are de - liv - - - ered
ihr seid ent - - gan - - - gen
of all cares that hold the world in
al - - ler Noth, die uns noch hält ge - -
cresc.
bond - - - - age. [Trs. M. D. Calvocoressi]
- fan - - - - gen.
(rit.)
Pedal
(m) f (16 & 8 ft.)

VII
O GOTT, DU FROMMER GOTT
O God, Thou faithful God

[Andante con moto]
MANUAL
(m)f Ch.
p Sw.
O
O
God, Thou faith - ful God,
Gott, du from - mer Gott,
(m)f Ch.
p Sw.
Thou Fount - ain ev - er
Du Brunn - quell al - ler

flow - - - ing,
Ga - - - ben,

R.H. (m)*f* Ch.

p Sw.

With - out whom no - thing is,
ohn den Nichts ist was ist,

(m)*f* Ch.

p Sw.

All per - fect
von dem wir

gifts be - - stow - - - ing,
al - - les ha - - - ben,
(m)f Gt.
R.H.
(m)f Gt.
p Sw. R.H.
L.H.
p Sw.
A
ge -
†(Gt. ad lib.)
pure and health - y frame
- sun - den Leib gib mir
(m)f Gt.
(Sw.)
p Sw.
O
und
†(Gt. ad lib.)
give me, and with - - in
dass in sol - chem Leib
(Gt.)
(Gt.)
(Sw.)
(m)f Ch.
(Gt.)
(Sw.)
(Sw.)
(Sw)

∗ The last R.H. note (E) on Gt. had better be omitted in performance.

† These two lines of the Chorale may be played on the Swell if preferred.

pSw.
A con - - science free from
ein un - - ver - - letz - - te
blame,
Seel'
(m)f Ch.
(m)f Sw. p
(dim.)
pp
A soul un - hurt by sin.
und rein Ge - wis - sen bleib.
[Trs. Edith M. Fowler]
R.H.
f Gt
(rit.)
Pedal
f 16 & 8 ft (Gt coupled)

VIII

ES IST EIN' ROS' ENTSPRUNGEN

Behold, a rose is blooming

[Andantino tranquillo]
Be - hold, a rose is bloom - - ing From
Es ist ein Ros' ent - sprun - - gen aus
MANUAL
p Ch.(or Gt.) dolce
out a ten - der root, Thus in the house of
ei - ner Wur - zel zart, wie uns die Al - ten
Sw.
Jes - - - se, As tell our an - - cient
sun - - - gen von Jes - - se war die
hymns, A young and ten - der shoot A -
Art, und hat ein Blüm - lein bracht mit -
Ch.(or Gt.)
R.H.

-mid the gloom of win - - - ter Burst
-ten im kal - - ten Win - - - ter wohl
forth in wond - -'rous bloom. [Trs. M. D. Calvocoressi]
zu der hal - - ben Nacht.
Sw.
(rit.)

IX

HERZLICH THUT MICH VERLANGEN

My heart is filled with longing

(1st SETTING)

[Moderato maestoso]
My heart is filled with long - - - - ing To
Herz - lich thut mich ver - lan - - - - gen nach
MANUAL
f Gt.
PEDAL
16 & 8 ft. (Gt. coupled)
pass a - way in peace;
ei - nem sel' - gen End,
For
weil
woes are round me throng - - - ing, And
ich hie bin um - fan - - - gen mit
tri - als will not cease.
Trüb - sal und E - lend.
Oh
Ich
Sw.
(mf)

(♪= ♪)
fain would I be hast - - - ing From
hab Lust ab - zu - schei - - - den von
p
thee, dark world of gloom, To
die - ser ar - gen Welt, seh
f Gt
glad - ness ev - er - last - - - ing; O
mich nach ew' - gen Freu - - - den, o
f Gt
f
Je - sus, quick - ly come! [Trs. Catherine Winkworth]
Je - su, komm nur bald!
(rit.)

X

HERZLICH THUT MICH VERLANGEN

My heart is filled with longing

(2nd SETTING)

[Lento grazioso]
MANUAL
p Sw. soft 8 & 4ft
molto legato
PEDAL
mp
Ch. soft 8ft Reed to Ped.
(no Pedal stops)
Herz - lich thut mich ver -
My heart is filled with
- lan - - gen nach ei - - nem sel' - - gen
long - - ing To pass a - way in

End,
peace;
weil
For
ich
woes
hie
are
bin
round
um - -
me
-fan - - - - -
throng - - - - -
gen
ing,
mit
And
Trüb - - -
tri - - -
sal
als
und
will
E - -
not

(♩=♩)
p Gt. (soft 8 ft. stop)
-lend.
cease.
Ich
Oh
hab Lust ab - zu - schei - - - den von
fain wou'l I be hast - - - ing From
(poco riten.)
(a tempo)
Sw.
die - ser ar - gen Welt,
thee, dark world of gloom,
più dolce sempre
sehn'
To

* Changes of manual are indicated at these points in the original Edition, but the manual parts may be played throughout on the Swell if preferred. In the latter case the suggested modification of phrasing given in dotted lines will be unnecessary.

mich nach ew' - - - - - gen
glad - - - - ness ev - - - - - er - - - -

riten. sempre
Freu - - - - - - - - den, O
- last - - - - - - - ing; O

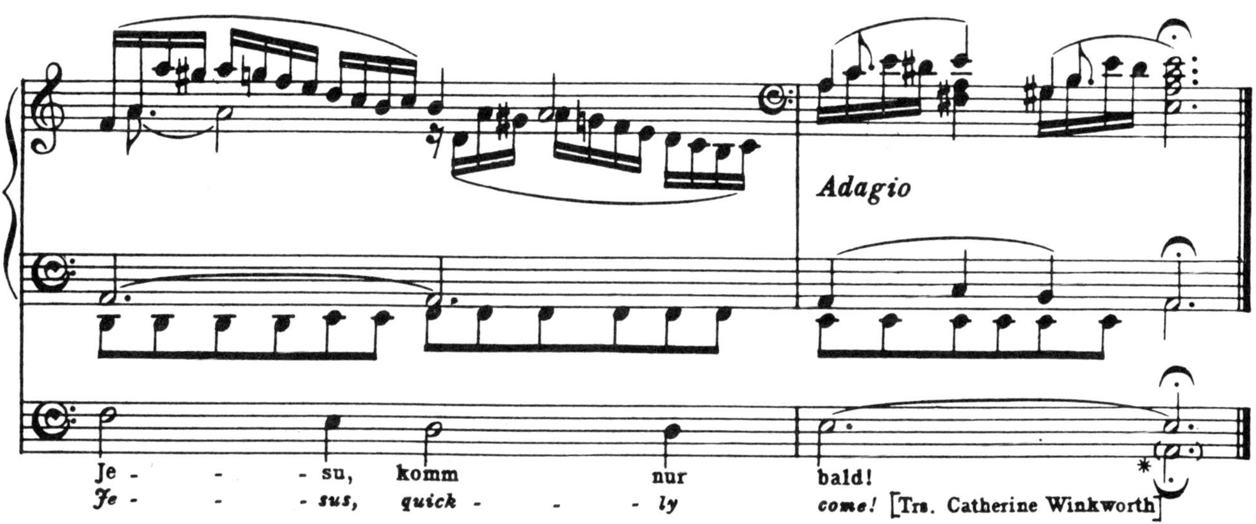
Adagio
Je - - - su, komm nur bald!
Je - - - sus, quick - - - ly come!
[Tr. Catherine Winkworth]

*It is recommended that the lower pedal note be omitted here.

XI

O WELT, ICH MUSS DICH LASSEN

O world, I now must leave thee

[Lento maestoso]
O world, I now must leave thee,
O Welt, ich muss dich las - sen,
MANUAL
Gt. f ma dolce (e legato)
p Ch.
PEDAL
f 16 & 8 ft. (Gt. coupled)
And go my lone - ly
ich fahr da - hin mein
pp Sw.
f Gt.
jour - ney
Stra - ssen
p Ch.
pp Sw.
To
ins
f Gt.

my e - ter - nal home.
ew'ge Va - ter - land.
p Ch.
pp Sw.
I faith - ful - ly and hum - bly
Mein Geist will ich auf - ge - ben,
f Gt
p Ch.
pp Sw.
Com - da -
f Gt
-mit my soul and bo - dy
-zu mein Leib und Le - ben
R.H.
p Ch.
L.H.

Un - to the Lord's all -
be - fehl'n in Got - tes
pp Sw.
R.H.
L.H.
f Gt

- lov - - - ing
gnäd' - - - ge
hands. [Trs. M.D. Calvocoressi]
Hand.
p Ch.
(16 ft in)

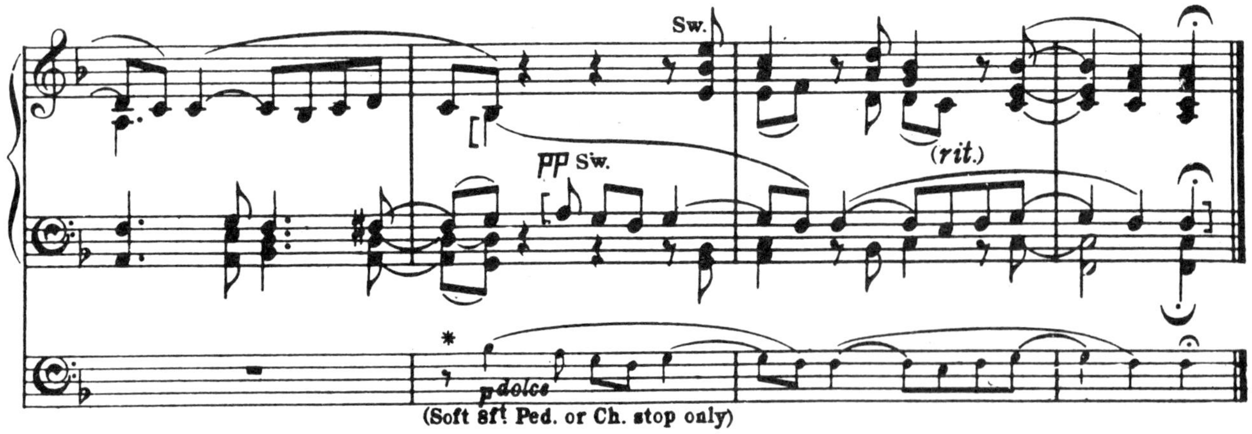
Sw.
pp Sw.
(rit.)
*
p dolce
(Soft 8ft Ped. or Ch. stop only)

* The small notes in the Pedal stave should be substituted for the melodic portion of the left hand part placed in brackets, if found practicable.

Printed and bound in Great Britain
by Headway Press Ltd

4/02 (44046)